CURIOSITIES OF
WEST YORKSHIRE

CURIOSITIES OF
WEST YORKSHIRE

ROBERT WOODHOUSE

First published in the United Kingdom in 2007 by
Sutton Publishing, an imprint of NPI Media Group Limited
Cirencester Road · Chalford · Stroud · Gloucestershire · GL6 8PE

British Library Cataloguing in Publication Data
A catalogue record for this book is available from the British Library.

ISBN 978-0-7509-4443-4

Typeset in Janson Text 11/13.5pt.
Typesetting and origination by Sutton Publishing
NPI Media Group Limited.
Printed and bound in England.

CONTENTS

VISITING THE CURIOSITIES

The curiosities covered in this book are to be found in a whole range of locations. Several are landmarks and these are perhaps best viewed from a distance (especially when close inspection may involve a demanding ascent). A number are privately owned (as domestic or business premises) and must be viewed from the roadside, while some are subject to normal opening times. During the summer months several of the properties are opened on a limited basis and details are usually available from local tourist information centres.

The curiosities can be visited either singly or in groups. A few are in fairly remote countryside and can only be reached on foot, but the large majority are accessible by public transport.

Due care and attention should be exercised, in terms of traffic, on public roads, and caution is required at locations beside canals.

ACKNOWLEDGEMENTS

Researching and composing material from such a wide geographical area has inevitably involved a considerable amount of travel by car, rail, canal and on foot. Before the actual visits to both rural and urban settings the initial step was to gather specific information about the structure itself and its location.

Apart from the author's own collection of books, articles and press cuttings, much information was gathered from local history departments at several libraries including Keighley, Northallerton, Otley, Bradford and Leeds. I am indebted to the local studies staff at these libraries for their diligence and expertise in locating and supplying information. Similar assistance was received from staff at tourist information centres at Leeds, Bradford, Wakefield, Settle, Halifax, Haworth, Huddersfield and Ilkley. Support on specific locations was provided by staff at Woodhouse Grove School, at Low Apperley, Gisburn Park Estate, the Landmark Trust and Shipley Glen Tramway.

Even with a map reference, some locations remained difficult to discover and it was on such occasions that traditional Yorkshire warmth and co-operation was in evidence. Local residents at Earby, Ilkley, Leeds, Low Bentham, Luddenden, Otley and the hamlet of Egypt proved to be invaluable in pointing out some less than obvious settings and there was similar support from church officials at St Andrew's Church, Kildwick, and the Old Grammar School Museum at Heptonstall.

Few major undertakings of this nature can be satisfactorily completed alone and a thank you is due to my wife, Sally, who showed her usual boundless enthusiasm in fulfilling a number of roles ranging from driver, navigator and map reader to research assistant and proof reader.

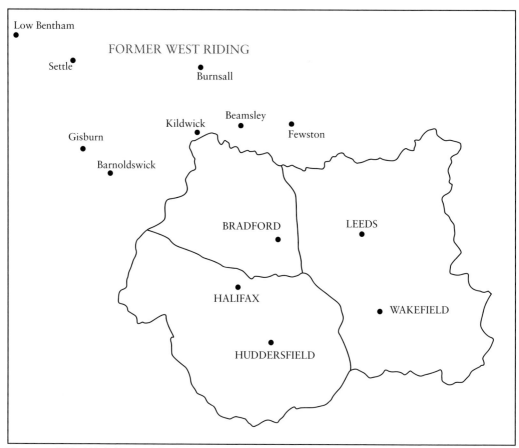

FORMER WEST RIDING

Low Bentham

Settle

Burnsall

Beamsley

Kildwick

Fewston

Gisburn

Barnoldswick

BRADFORD

LEEDS

HALIFAX

WAKEFIELD

HUDDERSFIELD

The area of West Yorkshire and the former West Riding covered by this book.

INTRODUCTION

West Yorkshire is well known for its mixture of spreading industrial settlements amid glorious natural landscapes, and these dramatic settings have influenced the nature and range of selected 'curiosities'. Upland slopes above Ilkley and Settle have provided the intriguing natural features of the Cow and Calf Rocks and Victoria Cave, and it was early inhabitants who left behind contrasting symbols in the form of Yeadon Stoop and the Swastika Stone, but most examples belong to more recent times.

Downtown industrial and municipal development brought not only the uniform outlines of mills and warehouses but also the amazing architectural features on buildings in central Leeds and Bradford. On a smaller scale, it is the actual location and layout of former industrial communities at Hebden Bridge and Heptonstall that provide interest and intrigue. One man's enterprise and initiative directed the development of a remarkable model township at Saltaire, and a range of civil engineering skills were employed in the construction of the amazing Bingley Five Rise Locks.

Churches and churchyards represent not only religious settings but are also a source of information about local events. It is the unusual length of Kildwick Church that creates interest, while Wakefield's chapel on the bridge is one of only four in the whole country (including one at nearby Rotherham). Churchyard memorials range from the poignant headstone of Lily Cove at Haworth to the powerful model of Bramhope tunnel in Otley churchyard.

Many of the summits in this area of Yorkshire are the sites for a range of towers and columns. Each one has a different story to tell and design features range from the simple outlines of towers at Cringle and Steeton to spectacular decorative detail on Wainhouse's Folly at Halifax.

The era of Victorian leisure pursuits and entertainment provided Ilkley's spa facilities including the intriguing bathhouse at 'White Wells', Bingley Glen Tramway and the harsh stonework of the Bear Pits at Leeds.

Little more than thirty years ago (in 1974) long-standing, traditional boundaries were redrawn in the interests of local government reorganisation. As a native Yorkshireman, I share the sadness of many other local folk at the passing of the county's three Ridings and for this reason I have included locations from the former West Riding which are now officially within North Yorkshire and Lancashire. Old allegiances and traditions are not easily forgotten and they have had a bearing on this chosen collection of 'curiosities'.

1

LEEDS & WAKEFIELD

CHARITY WITH MORE THAN A TOUCH OF SPLENDOUR

Aberford Almshouses

Quite a few villages have a set of almshouses where elderly or needy members of the community were accommodated, but few, if any, can match the architectural ostentatiousness of the Gascoigne Almshouses on the edge of Aberford village.

Stone-built in the Gothic style, they date from 1844 when George Fowler Jones's design features provided a whole array of gables and domed turrets on either side of a central tower complete with clock and canopied niches.

Such is the building's magnificence that it has been likened to a university college and when residents moved out a few years ago the interior space was converted into workshops for the City of Leeds Art Gallery.

Location: The almshouses are south of Aberford village (on the west side of the public road). Aberford is on the east side of Leeds about halfway to Tadcaster.

VICTORIAN TASTES IN ENTERTAINMENT

Bear Pits

A curious reminder of Victorian tastes in entertainment stands proudly on the southern side of Cardigan Road almost within throwing distance of the city's cricket ground. The impressive stonework has a mock castle frontage composed of two castellated turrets and a linking wall. Three barred entrances lead to the bears' den.

A plaque informs us that it was once part of the Leeds Zoological and Botanical Gardens and opened in 1840. Bears were exhibited in the circular pit and viewed from the top of the turrets (reached by spiral staircases).

This intriguing folly was acquired and restored in 1966 by Leeds Civic Trust but currently stands neglected and gathering litter.

Location: The Bear Pits are on the south side of Cardigan Road, close to the southern end of Headingley cricket and rugby ground.

ARCHITECTURAL GEMS IN AN INDUSTRIAL SETTING

Temple Mill, Tower Works and St Paul's House

The industrialisation of Leeds during the mid- to late nineteenth century added a multitude of factory roofs, chimneys, towers and warehouses to the city's spreading skyline. Functional structures with simple overall designs were the order of the day but here and there enlightened industrialists and designers erected buildings of outstanding merit.

Temple Mill in Marshall Street, south of the modern railway station, was built by Joseph Bonomi and James Combe for the owner, John Marshall. Bonomi had spent eight years in Egypt and this project, which cost Marshall around £250,000, was said to reflect the architecture of the temples at Karnak, Edfu and Dendera. Most prominent of the set of buildings (which were begun in 1837) is the administration block. It was added in 1843 and is trapeziform with winged emblems above the entrance and a portico with huge lotus flower capitals.

Inside, staircase railings were designed to look like bullrushes and office furniture was decorated with hieroglyphics. Towering over the works was a chimney that was shaped like Cleopatra's Needle.

It seems that there were few other commissions for Bonomi's Egyptian-style design work, with the only other notable examples being the spring at Hartwell House in Buckinghamshire and the Egyptian Court at Crystal Palace.

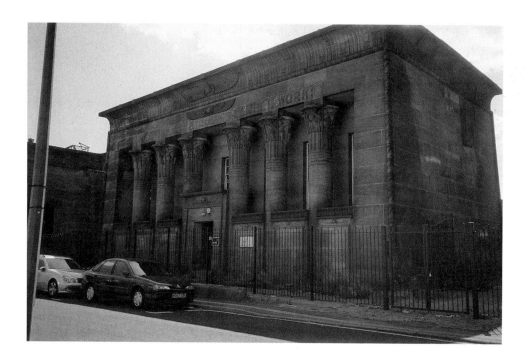

John Marshall showed commendable concern for the welfare of his employees and had sixty-six glass domes fitted into the roof in order to allow natural light to reach the workshop floor. In an attempt to provide a recreation area for the workforce Marshall sowed a lawn on the remainder of the roof space, and when the length of grass created problems he is said to have moved sheep to the upper level. Sadly, this proved to be an innovative move too far when some sheep fell through the domes.

Rapid industrialisation throughout much of West Yorkshire brought a rash of chimneys, towers and columns during the second half of the nineteenth century. Inevitably, there was a degree of drab repetition among these industrial landmarks, and in the late 1850s Sir Robert Rawlinson led a campaign to encourage more attractive designs for towers and chimneys. He found an ally in J.C. Loudon, a landscape designer, and because of their pressure Thomas Shaw, a Yorkshire architect, designed the first of the chimneys on the Globe Road site (south of Leeds railway station). Based on Lambert Tower in Verona, it was completed in 1864 for Harding & Son Ltd, a company that manufactured items such as combs, pins and cards for the textile industry.

A second, taller chimney was constructed during 1899 with design work by William Bakewell. He was influenced by Giotto's fourteenth-century marble bell tower of the Duomo in Florence and cleverly incorporated a section of the dust extraction plan within the soaring brick-built column. The ground-floor

boiler house was built as an acknowledgement of the work of notable textile engineers and has wall-mounted portrait medallions created by Alfred Drury.

The outstanding merit of these chimneys at the Tower Works resulted in substantial grants during the mid-1990s, and restoration work has ensured their future as a dramatic feature of Leeds' urban skyline.

St Paul's House occupies a central position close to Leeds City Square and takes its name from the Georgian church that formerly stood in nearby St Paul's Street. Its amazing design features were the work of Thomas Ambler who incorporated minarets, ornamental parapet and octagonal turrets within the fabric of this clothing factory.

The owner was John Barran, who transferred his business operations from London to Leeds during the 1840s. He successfully developed the mass production of ready-made clothing and recruited skilled workers from Russia when local labour was in short supply. This magnificent industrial building with its extraordinary Moorish features was totally renovated in 1977 to create 68,650sq.ft of office accommodation.

Location: Temple Mill is on the west side of Marshall Street to the south of the railway station. Tower Works are sited on the north side of Globe Road, close to the railway centre. St Paul's House is on the south side of Park Square fronting on to St Paul's Street.

REVEALING INSIGHT INTO A VICTORIAN BOOM TOWN

Beckett Street Cemetery, Leeds

By the beginning of the nineteenth century Leeds ranked as the seventh largest town in England. Some fifty years later the population of this major industrial centre stood at 172,258 and during the next few decades it became a town of many trades. Much of this growth was in the engineering industry and by 1860 this provided more employment for local men than did the textile trades. After 1870 the ready-made clothing industry expanded faster than other trades and by the end of Queen Victoria's reign some 300 small workshops were involved in the business.

This dramatic growth in industry was accompanied by a huge increase in population, which inevitably posed a range of social problems. Unsanitary conditions brought a rise in the mortality rate and this led Leeds Town Council to pioneer the English municipal cemetery on a site in Beckett Street during 1845.

Within the cemetery Anglicans and Dissenters were given their own chapels and areas for burial. A large number of other burials were in 'guinea graves', where a headstone and perimeter kerb enclosed a number of graves. The initial cost for one of these was £1 1s (with half price for children) but by 1921 the price had risen to £2.

Among the variety of monumental columns and memorials is a miniature factory chimney. It is said to be unique and serves as a tombstone for 'Thomas Kidney, the oldest steeplejack in England who died on November 17 1914 aged 82 years'.

Location: Beckett Street Cemetery is on the north-eastern side of the town centre opposite St James's Hospital.

A SHAM CASTLE IN DELIGHTFUL PARKLAND

Roundhay Park Castle

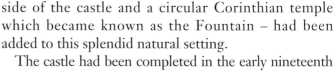

Roundhay Park covers some 800 acres of land on the north-eastern fringe of Leeds where John of Gaunt is said to have hunted during the late fourteenth century.

Historic features set out for Thomas Nicholson during the 1820s were the sham castle and a rustic hermitage, and in 1872 it was purchased by Leeds Corporation for the sum of around £140,000. HRH Prince Arthur performed the official opening after amenities – Cobble Hall, a large lodge on the east

side of the castle and a circular Corinthian temple which became known as the Fountain – had been added to this splendid natural setting.

The castle had been completed in the early nineteenth century on rising ground at the northern end of the park. It is composed of a square gatehouse with round corner towers. Cruciform arrow slits on either side of the pointed entrance provide a real sense of authenticity.

> *Location: Roundhay Park is on the north-eastern side of Leeds between the A58 (to the east) and the A6120 (to the north).*

YEADON STOOP

A Guidepost for Early Travellers

Yeadon Stoop (or Long Stoop) stands at a height of about 12ft beside a roundabout on the west side of the Leeds and Bradford Airport. No one can accurately date this tall stone column, which has an inscription stating that it was 'erected hundreds of years ago to guide travellers towards an ancient settlement at Dene Head to the east. It was moved from its earlier site 186 yards to the south west in the year 1984 for runway extensions.'

The positioning of this ancient pillar in the midst of modern traffic systems adds considerably to its impressive simplicity.

Location: Yeadon Stoop is situated on the west side of a roundabout on the A658 (west of Leeds and Bradford Airport).

THE BRAMHOPE MONUMENT

Otley Churchyard

The railway age of the mid-nineteenth century brought widespread changes to many aspects of Victorian society but the construction of the rail network took a heavy toll on human life.

A section of Otley churchyard, across Church Lane, has a scale model of the northern entrance to Bramhope railway tunnel which ran under the nearby Chevin. Construction work lasted from 1845 to 1849 and extended for some 2½ miles. During building operations accidents claimed the lives of twenty-three navvies and this highly unusual monument serves as a memorial to these fatalities.

Matching arches, each with a polygonal turret and a higher, round turret, are linked by a short length of tunnel. This striking reminder of the railway era stands around 6ft high and although there is no mention of the loss of life, the dedication includes prominent coverage of the contractor, James Bray, who paid for the memorial, and the surviving workforce.

> Location: *The Bramhope Monument is within All Saints' churchyard,*
> *close to the centre of Otley.*

AN UNUSUAL ARCH

Avenue des Hirondelles Arch

Occasionally unusual features retain their aura of mystery and intrigue and this is the case with an ornate stone-built archway on the A658, south of Pool. Inscribed with lettering which reads 'Avenue des Hirondelles' (hirondelle being the French for swallow), the arch is believed to date from about 1900 and leads to a driveway through woodland, but exhaustive efforts to uncover further background history have so far proved unsuccessful.

Location: The arch can be found along the A658 on the south side of Pool.

AN AMAZING ARRAY OF ANCIENT STONEWORK

St John's Church and Churchyard, Adel

T he tiny church of St John at Adel is largely unchanged since it was completed during the mid-twelfth century, and its many treasures include some outstanding examples of Norman stonework. Even older items of stonework in the adjacent churchyard serve to augment these incredible man-made stone features.

The south doorway was constructed between 1160 and 1180 at a time when Norman sculptural architecture was at its peak. A carved gable above the porch shows St John's vision of heaven through symbolic carvings of men and animals, while seven receding arches are highlighted by characteristic zigzag carving. A series of forty identical beaked heads decorate the inner arch around the door.

A series of seventy-eight corbels (projecting stone blocks) decorate the north, south and west walls in the form of grotesque heads and animals.

The chancel arch also dates from the mid-twelfth century and has a fascinating array of sculpture. Zigzag work features on the inner order, with a ladder running round the middle area and a whole assortment of beaked and bearded heads on the outer order. These include men with protruding tongues, a demon eating a child and others with animals in their jaws.

At the west end of the church the beautifully carved font cover was fashioned by Eric Gill. It was presented to the church in 1921 in memory of Alec Gordon, who died in 1916. The eight panels show six of the seven sacraments recognised by the twelfth-century church and form a splendid contrast with the earlier stonework.

Engravings linked with pagan worship have been excavated from the foundations of St John at Adel and may well indicate that the church was built over a pagan temple, as was often the case because the site was already sacred. A section of a broken pillar is set in the grassy area close to the west gate and displays patterning around the upper level.

Location: St John's Church is at the north end of Adel village, to the east of the A660.

A NATURAL SETTING FOR MAN-MADE CURIOSITIES

York Gate Garden at Adel

In recent years a quiet setting at York Gate in the village of Adel has been transformed into an incredible garden with a range of natural features. Water features, shady retreats and ornamental hedges merge among the greenery, which also shelters a whole collection of small-scale structures.

Unwanted stonework has been gathered here to create features such as an arbour with slate roof, stone classical tempietto (or mini-temple) and an open-roofed coroneted edifice with the grandiose title of 'The Folly'.

Location: York Gate Garden is adjacent to Back Church Lane at Adel, east of the A660 and about 6 miles north-west of Leeds city centre.

SERVING THE NEEDS OF TRAVELLERS FOR THE LAST SIX AND A HALF CENTURIES

Wakefield's Chantry Chapel of St Mary the Virgin

During the Middle Ages chapels on bridges were fairly commonplace, but changing townscapes have left just four in the whole of England. They were built partly as shrines to gather money for maintenance of the bridge. These splendid chantry chapels are still to be found at St Ives, Bradford-on-Avon, Rotherham and Wakefield where a nine-arched bridge crosses the River Calder.

Original building work on the Wakefield Chapel was completed in 1356, but as early as 1580 Camden described it as much defaced. During 1847 the façade was removed to Kettlethorpe Hall where it formed the frontage of a boathouse and restoration work on the chapel was carried out by Sir George Gilbert Scott in the same year. Further work on the west front was completed during 1939/40 by Sir Charles Nicholson using Derbyshire stone.

This replacement frontage is an exact copy of the original façade that was removed in 1847. Three of the five bays in the arcaded base have exquisite doorways with rich mouldings. Between the arches are pinnacled buttresses while the upper wall is covered with ornamental patterns. Scenes from the Annunciation, the Nativity, the Resurrection and Pentecost cover the area between canopied niches, while at the north-east corner of the chapel rises a turret which leads up to the roof and down steps to a small crypt.

The interior of the chapel has natural light from seven richly decorated windows and features of this delightful setting include an ornamental piscina and a charming niche close to the east window with a vaulted canopy.

During 2006 a series of events were organised by the Friends of Wakefield Chantry Chapel to mark the 650th anniversary of this remarkable building.

Location: The Chantry Chapel is on Wakefield Bridge at the south-east end of the town centre.

ECHOES OF THE DAYS BEFORE MODERN TRANSPORT SYSTEMS

Roadside Obelisk Marking Halfway Point

During recent years Leeds has consolidated its position as one of Britain's major business and commercial centres and a crucial factor in this area's success has been the network of modern road, rail and air links.

Each working day, thousands of commuters pass a reminder of an earlier era in the shape of a roadside obelisk near Kirkstall Abbey. A stone-built pillar on the south side of the A65 marks the halfway point between the capital cities of England and Scotland and dates from the days before a national railway network and powered flights.

A tablet on the column reads:

> To London 200 miles
> To Edinburgh 200 miles
> Erected AD 1829
> B & B
> Kirkstall Forge 1779
> Leeds 3½ miles

Location: The obelisk can be seen on the south side of the A65 between Leeds centre and Horsforth, about 4 miles from the city centre and slightly west of Kirkstall Abbey.

2

BRADFORD

REMARKABLE DESIGNS HIGHLIGHTING BRADFORD'S VICTORIAN SPLENDOUR

City Hall, Wool Exchange, Yorkshire Penny, Church Institute and No. 30 Chapel Street

During the first half of the nineteenth century Bradford was transformed from a rural township surrounded by woods and fields into a spreading industrial settlement covering a large part of the Aire Valley.

Old buildings in the town centre were replaced by new business premises using local sandstone and with design work by prominent local designers and builders. Many of these amazing Victorian structures with their wide range of sculptural ornamentation remain at the heart of Bradford's central area.

When the present city hall was opened in 1873, Bradford was still a town but expanded during the early 1900s after city status was granted in 1897. Bradford's dominant feature is a soaring clock tower, designed along the lines of a Tuscan campanile, and the upper levels are highlighted by thirty-five carved figures of British monarchs. Each one is 7ft tall and this splendid array

of royalty surprisingly includes Oliver Cromwell. Statues of Queen Elizabeth I and Victoria stand proudly on either side of the main entrance. The building was recently used as a courthouse for the trial of Tracey Barlow on TV's *Coronation Street*.

The architects who designed the city hall, Lockwood and Mawson, also worked on the Wool Exchange (1867) where the sculptor, James Tolmie, included a whole series of historical figures. Below the clock tower are the figures of Bishop Blaise, patron saint of wool combers, and King Edward III, who gave strong support to the wool trade. Along the adjoining wall are portraits of politicians, industrialists and celebrated historical figures. This splendidly imposing building is topped with highly decorative roof parapets and pinnacles which boldly demonstrate the prosperity and prestige that

Bradford had gained from the wool trade by the 1860s.

There are more carved figures on the Yorkshire Penny Bank building (of 1895) which portray important characters from the bank's early years, while the topmost section overflows with an elaborate collection of figures and horns of plenty in the Renaissance grotesque style.

On a smaller scale, the Church Institute in North Parade (built 1871–3) has a prominent display of arches and pinnacles as well as roundel portraits of Archbishop Sharpe (1644–1713) and Bishop Blaise. Ranged along the roof line are dragons supporting shields, while symbolic beasts peer outwards from above first-floor windows.

Across the city centre, on Chapel Street, no. 30 has a number of sculptured keystone heads with unknown origins. It has been suggested that they may be linked to countries that the warehouse owner traded with, or possibly continents, but the truth behind these strange carvings remains a mystery.

Location: City Hall is at the bottom of Sunbridge Road; the Wool Exchange is at the northern end of Market Street; the Yorkshire Penny Bank is at the junction of North Parade and Manor Row; the Church Institute is on North Parade and Chapel Street is between Leeds Road and Peckover Street.

A STRIKING LINK BETWEEN BRADFORD'S PAST AND PRESENT

The Ivegate Arch

The Bradford area was probably engaged in ironworking during the Roman period and an early community dating from Saxon times had grown into a small township by the Middle Ages. Wool production brought prosperity from the fourteenth century but upheavals during the Civil War brought a serious decline in the town's fortunes.

It was worsted production during the first half of the nineteenth century that brought a rapid upturn in Bradford's fortunes. Coal mining, iron smelting and machine manufacturing added to the town's dramatic growth as the population

leapt from 6,400 in 1801 to 104,000 by 1851. A whole range of business and commercial premises were constructed in local sandstone and though a recent phase of redevelopment has brought modern and innovative features to the city centre many of the outstanding Victorian buildings remain.

Ivegate is one of the oldest streets in Bradford and dates back some 500 years. It formerly led to a manor house, coaching inn, prison and court house. During 1988 an innovative arch was constructed at the junction of Ivegate and Market Street with panels representing aspects of the city's industrial, sporting and cultural past. Buildings such as Bradford Cathedral, the city hall and National Media Museum (formerley the National Museum of Photography, Film and Television) are featured along with celebrities including Frederick Delius and J.B. Priestley, while other panels recall aspects such as the locality's strong rugby and brass band traditions.

This splendid representation of Bradford's varied heritage was designed and constructed by members of a group of local artists and blacksmiths named the Fire and Iron Design Group.

Location: The Ivegate Arch is located at the junction of Market Street and Ivegate to the north of the city hall.

A MODEL IDEA THAT JUST GREW AND GREW

Saltaire

Titus Salt was born at Morley, near Leeds, on 20 September 1803, and as he reached adulthood a capacity for hard work and innovation coupled with a reputation for punctuality and thrift made him the mainstay of the firm of Daniel Salt & Son (Wool Staplers). During the 1820s he visited wool sales in London and Liverpool as well as arranging direct purchases from farmers in Norfolk and Lincolnshire.

During the following decade it was Salt's willingness to innovate and experiment that opened up productive new areas of business. At the age of twenty-eight Titus Salt imported Donskoi wool from Russia, yet was unable to sell it as the coarse and tangled fibres were not easy to work. He therefore decided to spin it himself and went on to build his own mill to process it. This was followed by an even more profitable venture with a consignment of 300 bales of alpaca wool that was landed at Liverpool dock in 1836.

By the 1840s Salt was operating five mills in the Bradford area and his pioneering approach led to experiments with mohair, which was then used to cover seats in railway carriages. Titus Salt's original plans included retirement at the age of 50 in order to pursue a rural lifestyle, but a number of events during the late 1840s brought a change of plan.

In 1848, during a period of Chartist agitation for improved housing conditions and the right to vote, he was elected as the second mayor for Bradford. An outbreak of cholera during 1849 added to the area's troubles.

Salt used his qualities as a businessman and humanitarian to set up a new settlement in the Aire Valley. Saltaire took shape over some twenty-five years and Titus Salt negotiated the purchase of land as the scheme progressed. Workers at Salt's mill were housed in streets that were named after Queen

Victoria, Prince Albert, Salt himself, his wife Caroline, the architects and his children and grandchildren. By 1871 Saltaire had 823 houses and a population of 4,389, with the overall housing scheme taking some fourteen years to complete. Most residents of Saltaire were employed at the mill which opened on Titus Salt's fiftieth birthday (20 September 1853) with design features

aimed at overcoming the danger of fire and accidents. It represented the first fully integrated textile mill with all operations under a single roof and facilitated production of about 18 miles of cloth each day.

As the village expanded a whole range of amenities were added including schools, churches, a club and institute, infirmary and shops. The New Mill was constructed to the north of the earlier mill during 1868 and Salt's concern that its chimney would spoil the view down Victoria Road led to the inclusion of a campanile copied from the Venetian church of Santa Maria Gloriosa.

Throughout the village was the guiding influence of Titus Salt. From lettering above the windows of the splendid Italian-style Congregational church (of 1859) to rules for the club (and institute) and the bath and wash houses, residents were made aware of the principles and values of this amazing Victorian businessman and benefactor.

Titus Salt died on 29 December 1876 and the business and village came under the control of Titus jnr, but following his death in 1887 decline set in and Saltaire was sold to a consortium. Deterioration continued through the twentieth century, until the 1980s brought an upturn in the village's fortunes. Formation of the Saltaire Village Society in 1984 led to recognition of the area's outstanding status. The railway station was reopened and housing was upgraded during the mid-1980s before Jonathan Silver bought the mill in 1987 and gave it a new lease of life as a base for businesses and galleries. During the 1990s regeneration continued with restoration of the Victoria Hall and the former Factory Schools (as Shipley College). In spite of the death of Jonathan Silver in 1997 his plans for further canal-side development have continued and in 1999 this splendid aspect of nineteenth-century social and economic history was nominated for World Heritage Status.

Location: Saltaire is on the north side of the A650 (between Bingley and Shipley), about 4½ miles north of Bradford.

STILL GOING STRONG: BRITAIN'S OLDEST WORKING CABLE TRAMWAY

Shipley Glen Tramway

During the Victorian era Shipley Glen's natural beauty drew increasing numbers of visitors from West Yorkshire. In the 1880s further attractions were added in the form of a switchback railway and a type of camera obscura before local businessman, Sam Wilson, opened a tramway on 18 May 1895. He soon brought other attractions to the area including a steam launch on the nearby Leeds and Liverpool Canal, and thousands of visitors flocked to the Vulcan House Tea Rooms and the Pleasure Gardens.

During the 1920s and '30s new owners, the Parr family, brought prosperity to the tramway before selling out to a company named Glen Tramways Limited. George Rushton was employed as manager and a further period of popularity followed before holidaymakers began to look further afield for leisure outings.

Public holidays still brought large numbers of tourists to Shipley Glen but on Whitsuntide Monday 1966 the tramway came to a juddering halt when tramcars overran the platform ends. Thankfully there were no serious injuries but the situation worsened when vandals and thieves placed the future of the Glen Tramway in serious doubt.

Local residents and business owners rallied round and a new company, Glen Enterprises Limited, was set up to resurrect this amazing example of late Victorian engineering. The tramway began to operate again in June 1969 but further difficulties brought the end of Glen Enterprises' involvement at Easter 1981 and ownership passed to Bradford Metropolitan Council.

Operations were taken over by Bradford Trolleybus Association on 23 January 1982 and during May 1995 a centenary event featured a half-size replica of the front section of a tram, photographic displays and a small-scale museum. On 1 January 2003 operations were taken over by the Glenway Tramway Preservation Co. Ltd and a team of volunteers have continued to operate the tramway and improve facilities at both ends of the incline.

This remarkable Victorian attraction is the oldest working tramway in Britain. The tramway has a gauge of 20in running along two tracks with a pair of toast-rack trams on each line and offers a splendidly nostalgic link between Saltaire and the elevated vantage point above Shipley Glen.

The tramway is open most weekends and Bank Holiday afternoons throughout the year.

Location: Shipley Glen Tramway is on the north side of the River Aire between Bingley and Baildon.

A WATER-FILLED STAIRCASE OF AMAZING PROPORTIONS

Bingley Five Rise Locks

During the second half of the eighteenth century rapid industrial growth in the north and in the Midlands resulted in the growth of a network of canals. Foodstuffs and raw materials were shipped into these spreading conurbations and manufactured products shipped out.

The Leeds and Liverpool Canal took around forty years to complete at a total cost of about £1.5 million. In 1773 the section from Gargrave to Shipley was opened and four years later this broad, man-made waterway reached Leeds. The final stretch that extended to Liverpool was completed in 1816 and this 127-mile-long canal was fed with water from several streams as well as reservoirs near Winterburn, Barrowford and Rishton.

Locks were necessary to allow boats to move up or down an incline in a controlled manner and at some locations staircase locks were needed to cope with sudden changes in gradient.

Bingley Five Rise Locks are probably the best known and most used staircase locks in British Waterways. The opening day in 1774 was accompanied by a peal of church bells, band music and gunfire and a plaque on the lock house wall gives details of its dimensions: 'Open 21 March 1774, Engineer John Longbottom of Halifax, Built by local stonemasons Barnabas Morvil, Jonathan Farrar, and Wm Wild of Bingley and John Sugden, of Wilsden, Rise 59 ft 2in in 320ft, 16 miles 2 furlongs to Leeds, 111 miles to Liverpool.'

The Leeds and Liverpool Canal played a major role in developing industries on both sides of the Pennines and down the years a wide range of cargoes were transported through the lock systems. Large quantities of coal, wool and limestone were moved by horse-drawn 'short boats' (measuring some 60ft by

14ft) before cocoa and dried fruit (bound for York's chocolate factories), sugar (from Tate & Lyle's Liverpool works) and cement from the Humber area became regular cargoes.

During the second half of the nineteenth century the growth of a national railway network followed by a decline in traditional industries and the spread of cheap road transport led to a downturn in canal traffic. In 1948 the canal was included in a nationalisation scheme but after suffering years of decline throughout the 1960s and '70s canals have re-emerged under British Waterways management as a popular leisure and recreational resource.

On the approach to Bingley Five Rise from Bingley railway station the towpath passes a shorter version, the Three Rise Locks (about half a mile away) while a nearby lock cottage has another curious feature. The cottage walls include brick with a series of random letters of the alphabet. These recycled bricks were brought from a demolished warehouse in Liverpool and during construction of the cottage they were not reused in their original order. With careful observation it is possible to pick out the individual letters that make up the words Leeds and Liverpool Canal Co.

Location: The best approach to the locks is along the towpath from Bingley station and Park Road (though a minor road, Beck Lane, leads directly to the top lock).

ALL QUIET ON THE STANBURY FRONT

The Old Silent Inn, Stanbury

There is many a good yarn behind most pub names and the Old Silent Inn at Stanbury boasts a most unusual tale. Originally named the Eagle, this isolated hostelry was allegedly renamed the Old Silent Inn after Bonnie Prince Charlie spent time in hiding there and trusted local residents to keep quiet during his stay.

During the nineteenth century a landlady reportedly fed the stray cats that roamed wild on adjacent moorland. She is said to have attracted them by ringing a bell in the doorway of the inn. Reports suggest that the bell can still be heard ringing out on wild winter nights and recent landlords claim to have been pestered by numbers of cats.

Location: Old Silent Inn is at the west end of Stanbury, some 2½ miles west of Haworth (between Keighley Moor and Haworth Moor).

PART FOLLY, PART PARK, PART BOWLING GREEN

Oakworth Park

Most towns and cities have municipal parks but few can claim to include such an unusual layout as Oakworth Park near Keighley. Originally the site was covered by a mansion and grounds belonging to Sir Isaac Holden (1807–97), an inventor and textile millionaire. He spent lavishly on the construction of a winter garden which included a Turkish bath which cost anything between £30,000 and £120,000. Although the winter garden has long since disappeared, most of the adjacent parkland remains largely intact.

Around the only surviving section of the mansion – the portico – is a curious arrangement of caves, grottoes and passageways. The work was carried out

between 1864 and 1867 by a specialist French labour force using a method of iron-reinforced moulded concrete and includes a summerhouse, grand cascade and fossil tree (with a flight of steps leading to a high level walkway above the spreading walls, branches and leaves).

Amid this strange assortment of rustic features and on the site of the mansion there is now a bowling green.

Location: Oakworth Park is on the north side of the B6143 close to the centre of the village of Oakworth between Haworth and Keighley.

HAWORTH'S HIDDEN SECRET

A Mortuary Stone in Haworth

Haworth's connections with the Brontë family attract multitudes of visitors every year. Although many tourists call in at the Tourist Information Centre few, if any, will be aware of the building's chequered past.

Below the TIC lies a small low-roofed cellar which is now used as a storage area. In earlier days it is believed that it served as a mortuary with corpses transported from their deathbeds to dissecting tables through a low side entrance on Changegate.

On the left-hand side of the building is a sunken tunnel which led to a communal well, while at pavement level a large slab (underneath the traffic notice) is a relic from the nearby children's mortuary.

Location: Haworth TIC is in the centre of the village which is about 6 miles south-west of Keighley.

TRAGIC OUTCOME TO A BALLOONING FEAT

Lily Cove

Cemeteries are an invaluable source of information about many aspects of local life. Among the epitaphs and eulogies are countless details – often poignant, sometimes amusing – about people and events.

A simple inscription on a dark gravestone at Haworth cemetery recalls sad events at the local gala in June 1906 which led to the death of Lily Cove.

Reports in the *Keighley Herald* for Saturday 16 June 1906 describe Miss Cove's burial two days earlier following a tragic accident on 11 June. Lily Cove from East London had stayed at the White Lion Hotel in Haworth before her

appearance at the gala. She had been employed by the pioneering aeronaut, Captain Bidmead, to make a parachute jump from a gas-filled balloon, but the performance was postponed on 9 June because of a lack of breeze and shortage of gas in the balloon.

Some 7,000 people gathered two days later to watch the huge balloon rise easily and then drift towards Stanbury Moor. At a height of about 600 or 700ft Lily Cove jumped from the balloon but she failed to activate her parachute and plummeted to the ground near Ponden Reservoir. She died from her injuries within a few minutes.

Investigators concluded that Miss Cove unhooked her parachute because she was a non-swimmer and feared that she was heading for the reservoir, but in fact her altitude was not as low as she estimated.

Location: Lily Cove's grave is in the new cemetery to the south of Haworth. It is just ahead and to the right of the main entrance.

A QUEEN OF WATERING PLACES AMID A STRANGE ASSORTMENT OF STONE CARVINGS

Ilkley's Spa, Cow and Calf Rocks and the Swastika Stone

Between the 1840s and early 1900s visitors from industrial settings at Leeds and Bradford flocked to the Heather Spa of Ilkley. Spa buildings spread towards high ground above the town where Victorian health seekers could marvel at early moorland carvings.

Roman legions had a base (named Olicana) spreading over some two acres around the site of the present parish church. The garrison was abandoned late in the third century and early visitors were no doubt intrigued by the clay ramparts of the encampment before they set off to explore the surrounding moorland.

One of the earliest spas was located at White Wells above Wells Road, where a curious group of white-walled rooms includes a plunge pool.

Rocks and boulders on moorland around Ilkley demonstrate numerous examples of Bronze Age carvings. Most are variations of the 'cup and ring' motif showing an engraved free-standing ring or a ring enclosing a central hollow 'cup', but the exact meaning of these strange designs remains unclear. Experts believe that 'cup and ring' motifs date back to the early Bronze Age and at locations such as Baildon Moor and Addingham High Moor there are adjacent Bronze Age circles and earthworks.

Rombalds Moor sweeps around the south side of Ilkley at a height of more than 1,300ft above sea level and is covered with a range of prehistoric remains including hut circles, round barrows, cairns, rock engravings, field systems, entrenchments and enclosures.

Closer to Ilkley, at the eastern edge of Ilkley Moor, is the massive bulk of the Cow and Calf Rocks whose curious natural outlines attract hordes of sightseers. Access to the moor top and the rocks is by the aptly named Cowpasture Road, and from the summit views take in the peaks of Ingleborough and Whernside as well as the Vale of York, Fountains Abbey and moorland around Settle.

At one time there was an additional rocky outcrop, the Bull Rock, but it was broken up and used for building stone.

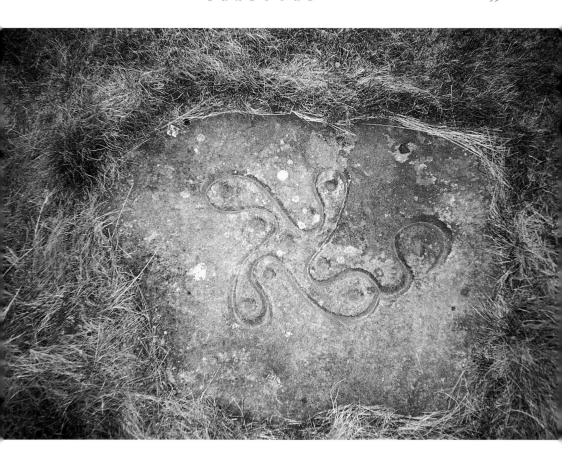

Above the western edge of Ilkley, close to the charming wooded ravine of Heber's Ghyll, is perhaps the strangest of all the carvings in the area. It takes the form of a curved swastika, a commonly used motif in Celtic art, which is a symbol of fire and may well date from the Iron Age.

Location: Ilkley is located on the A65 between Skipton and Otley. The Cow and Calf rocks are prominent on high ground at the south-east end of the town and the Swastika Stone is just beyond Heber Ghyll at the south-west edge of the township. White Wells bath house is immediately south of Ilkley and is open to the public when the flags are flying.

LANDMARKS GALORE –
OF ALL SHAPES AND SIZES

Lund's Tower and Wainman's Pinnacle

From mill chimneys to monumental towers, West Yorkshire has almost a preponderance of distinctive landmarks – and two are found in close proximity on Sutton Moor, to the west of Keighley.

Lund's Tower, a square castellated structure, has been given a number of local names ranging from 'Jubilee' and 'Ethel's' to 'Salt Pot'. It was built on land belonging to Buxton Farm between 1890 and 1892 with stone transported

from a quarry in nearby Hangingstone Lane. Masons were brought from Cowling, Sutton and Buxton Farm. The cost of construction was met by James Lund of Malsis Hall and the completed structure incorporated a spiral staircase with thirty-nine steps leading to a balcony that provided views across Airedale.

Inevitably, the ravages of time have taken a toll on this appealing column but during 1974 the Crosshills Naturalists' Society carried out repairs and pointing work and later, after the tower had passed into the care of Sutton-in-Craven Parish Council in 1997, the Sutton Conservation Group completed further renovations.

The nearby Wainman's Pinnacle is believed to have been set up in memory of Richard Wainman who died in the Napoleonic Wars. Other theories suggest that it is a celebration of victory at Waterloo or a memorial to a member of the Wainman family killed in the Civil War.

Location: Lund's Tower and Wainman's Pinnacle are on Sutton Moor to the west of Keighley, above the villages of Sutton and Cowling.

MOORTOP REMINDER OF AN ENGINEERING PROJECT

The Old Tower at Cringles

This slender, soaring structure is located on Rombalds Moor, to the north of Silsden. Initial impressions suggest a link with mineral workings but it was in fact erected as a survey tower during construction work on the Barden aqueduct.

Some 5 miles to the east (south of Ilkley) there used to be a similar landmark at Thimble Stones, this time a hunting tower, close to the highest point of this spreading moorland.

Location: Cringles Old Tower is on the west side of the A6034, 2 miles north of Silsden.

AN IMPRESSIVE MONUMENT

Steeton Tower

S teeton Tower stands four storeys high and rises some 70ft above an adjacent private wood and paddock. It is rather larger than most similar structures and was constructed between 1897 and 1901 by local mill owner Henry Isaac Butterfield in the same style as his Keighley residence, Cliffe Castle. Built to celebrate Queen Victoria's Golden Jubilee, it was completed just before her death and later became the home for the gamekeeper of Henry's son, Sir Frederick Butterfield.

This impressive monument looks out across the Aire Valley but during the latter part of the twentieth century has remained unoccupied. In 1997 new owners replaced timbers and rebuilt turrets, and following a further change of ownership during 2003 the tower remains in private hands.

Location: Steeton Tower is on the north side of a minor road linking Steeton and Utley (on the north-west edge of Keighley).

A QUAKER'S TOWER

Elam's Tower

The Manor of Lower Woodhouse covers land on the north-east side of Bradford close to the River Aire. It was purchased by Robert Elam in 1799 and under his direction a round pagoda-style structure was replaced by a square tower. Mr Elam belonged to a Quaker charity and

between 1799 and 1804 unemployed menfolk from nearby Apperley Bridge were involved in construction work. With Mr Elam supervising building operations using stone from a quarry at Rawdon, it is reported that the workforce received fair wages and conditions.

For some time the tower was used to store water and floors remained intact until the 1950s. A pathway led to the summit of this man-made mount and it served as an observatory. In more recent times Elam's Tower has become derelict, and though the slopes are covered in dense undergrowth they still support a glorious display of bluebells in springtime.

Location: Elam's Tower is within the grounds of Woodhouse Grove School in Apperley Bridge on the north side of the River Aire and east of the A658.

WHAT'S IN A NAME?
FROM EGYPT TO TRIANGLE

Unlikely and Unusual Local Place Names

Every area has its own collection of strange place names and West Yorkshire is no exception. Often the origin of these unlikely names has been lost in the mists of time and we are left to rely on speculative conjecture but in some cases there are firmer links to local events and personalities.

Scapegoat Hill, Toot Hill and Catherine Slack have no known connections but there are possible links between the origins of Egypt, a hamlet west of Bradford,

and the Battle of the Nile during the period of the Napoleonic Wars. Local quarrymen constructed grit walls along the roadside which gained them the rather exaggerated title of the Walls of Jericho (but these have now disappeared).

Gooseye may have its origins in an old English word meaning land among streams or 'Goose hey' meaning a meadow or field in which geese are fed.

Triangle may derive its name from an inn of the same name that was built on a three-sided plot of land in the locality and although there are no clues to the origins of Friendly, it is hard to believe that local people are anything other than a convivial group.

Location: Egypt is north of the B6145, 6 miles west of Bradford. Gooseye is 3½ miles west of Keighley on the North Beck. Triangle is on the A58, 6 miles south-west of Halifax.

3

HUDDERSFIELD
& HALIFAX

RAILWAY ARCHITECTURE ON THE CLASSICAL SCALE

Huddersfield Railway Station

The mid-Victorian railway boom produced a whole range of fine buildings but Huddersfield station ranks as one of the most exceptional of this country's early railway buildings.

J.P. Pritchett designed the splendid classical features of this amazing structure which dates from 1848–9 and was the work of a local mason Joseph Kaye. It has all the appearance of a grand city hall with a central portico and colonnades at each side. Corinthian columns range across the middle section and along the spreading wings, while the British Rail insignia is displayed prominently over the portal.

> *Location: Huddersfield railway station lines the western side of St George's Square in the centre of the town.*

CHEQUERED CAREER FOR A FORMER CHURCH

Queen Street Methodist Chapel

When it was first opened in 1819 Huddersfield's Queen Street Methodist Chapel was said to be the largest Wesleyan Mission building in the world. A splendid classical façade made up a section of this impressive roadway which was completed between 1820 and 1830 and also included the County Court.

The interior accommodated almost 2,000 worshippers but closure in 1970 brought a very different usage. For a time it operated as an arts centre before it was transformed into a squash club called The Ridings with an adjacent nightclub named The Catacombs. A further change of use in the mid-1990s has seen it returned to the arts world as the Lawrence Batley Theatre. The central auditorium occupies the former chapel area while a smaller Cellar Theatre and restaurant are housed in the south wing where the superintendent minister used to live.

> Location: Lawrence Batley Theatre is prominent on the north side of Queen Street in central Huddersfield.

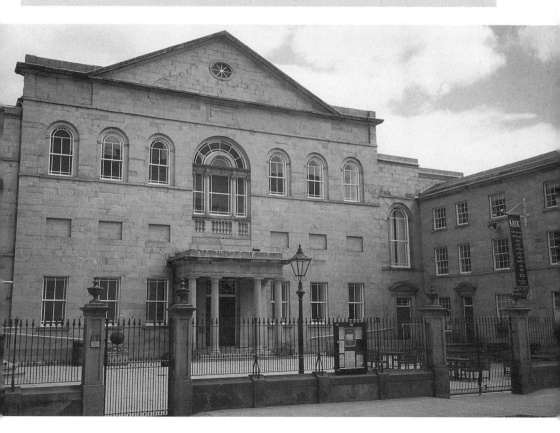

NO SHORT MEASURES AT THE TINIEST OF BARS

Huddersfield Hotel

The Huddersfield Hotel occupies a prominent position in the centre of the town. Just a few years ago there were eight bars and four cellars in the area behind an impressive frontage, but it was the tiniest of all bars that caught the attention.

A red telephone kiosk was opened as a bar in May 1985 despite objections from the local fire officer who was concerned about the lack of an emergency exit. This mini bar was recognised by the *Guinness Book of Records* as the smallest bar in the world.

In recent years the Huddersfield Hotel became part of the Swallow Hotel Group but in the late summer of 2006 Swallow Hotels were placed into receivership.

Location: The Huddersfield Hotel is on the west side of Kirkgate, close to the Market Place.

ALMS FOR THE POOR . . .
SOME THREE CENTURIES
DOWN THE LINE

Old Tristram

St John's Church at Halifax was heavily restored during the nineteenth century but retains many of its original features such as fourteenth-century windows from earlier phases of building work. It also houses a striking life-size effigy of an old man with a bushy beard wearing a long coat and breeches.

He is widely known as 'Old Tristram', although he has also been referred to as 'Trosteram', a member of a local shoe-making family. There is disagreement about the date of the effigy for although an inscription includes the date 1701 the style of clothing suggests that it could have been a century earlier. Opinion seems to agree that Old Tristram was licensed to beg around the streets of Halifax and in the church porch on behalf of the poor of the parish.

Some three centuries down the line this striking figure is still collecting alms for the poor.

Location: St John's Church is adjacent to Cripplegate and Church Street on the east side of Halifax town centre.

SOLE SURVIVOR FROM THE HALCYON DAYS OF DOMESTIC CLOTH MAKING

Piece Hall, Halifax

Domestic cloth making had become established in the Halifax area of West Yorkshire by the medieval period, with farming families supplementing a meagre income by producing lengths of cloth. These 'pieces' of cloth were usually 30yds in length and had a width determined by the sideways spread of the loom.

Finished pieces of woven cloth were transported into local towns for sale at market and Halifax may well have been the first town to open a cloth hall (on a site near Waterhouse Street) in 1572. As other textile towns prospered, and with new halls taking shape at centres such as Colne, Wakefield and Leeds, a public meeting was held at the Talbot Hotel, Halifax, on 9 April 1774 to discuss plans for a new market building.

A wealthy local landowner's offer of a site on Talbot Close was chosen by the planners, and the architect for the new Piece Hall is believed to have been John Hope of Liverpool. A rectangular building took shape around a central courtyard of about 10,000sq. yd and in order to create a constant roof level on the sloping site an extra storey was added on the east (lower) side. Aspects of Roman classical architecture were incorporated in the form of huge rustic piers supporting semicircular arches on the ground floor, known as the 'arcade level', square joined columns on the 'rustic level' and a continuous sequence of circular Doric columns along the top floor or 'colonnade'.

Each corner of Piece Hall has an internal staircase and there are entrances on the north, south and west sides. The North Gate has its original studded oak plank door while the South Gate has a pair of ornate cast-iron gates that display the Halifax coat of arms. The gates were installed in 1871 when part of the colonnade was removed to give extra height for vehicular access.

Around the courtyard were 315 numbered rooms, each one measuring about 12ft by 8ft and including a door and a window. Records indicate that most

tenants came from the Calderdale area around Halifax but others were based in Bradford, Burnley, Keighley and Skipton.

Piece Hall prospered for around thirty-five years before greater mechanisation of the textile industry affected the position of handloom weavers. By the mid-nineteenth century merchants were buying from mills where the textile processes had been brought under one roof. By the early 1830s fewer than 200 rooms in Piece Hall were in use, but the building had found an alternative use as a venue for political and social activities.

The first of these social gatherings probably took place in June 1816 when Don Pedro paid a £5 fee in order to display his fireworks, and during January 1820 officers and troops from the 6th Regiment of Foot assembled here at the time of the Luddite riots. At Whitsuntide 1831 the Sunday School Union held its Jubilee 'Sing' and these 'Sings' continued every five years until 1890, crowds growing in size from 10,000 (in 1831) to 30,000 at the final event.

Other notable events held at Piece Hall during the mid-nineteenth century included the first Yorkshire Band Contest on 26 August 1854 when Dewsbury Band took first prize, a celebration on 29 May 1856 to mark peace with Russia,

and a service attended by about 6,000 people where the Revd C.H. Spurgeon was the preacher. There was another spellbinding event at Piece Hall on 23 August 1861 when the world-famous tightrope walker Charles Blondin crossed the central quadrangle, from corner to corner, at a height of about 60ft. Musical accompaniment for his daring feat, which took place soon after his crossing of Niagara Falls, was provided by the Black Dyke Mills Band.

Unexpected drama followed two years later when a manned balloon ascent went badly wrong on 12 September 1863. An expectant crowd waited for hours for the balloon to be fully inflated only for it to be caught in telegraph wires above Piece Hall. After release from the wires it narrowly cleared the nearby roof before becoming stuck on the high chimney of Firth & Son's Mill. As the balloon punctured, the car was left hanging 120ft above the ground as the owner (and balloonist) a Mr Youngis, clambered down a rope to safety.

For more than a century there were few social events in Piece Hall but, after its classification as an ancient monument in July 1928, there was a range of suggestions for its future use. These included a car park, a sports centre, children's hospital, a Garden of Remembrance and an open-air swimming pool.

It was only when the government offered financial assistance that moves were made to safeguard the future of Piece Hall, which had Grade I listing and ranked as the last of its kind in the country. Renovation work involved the opening of an industrial textile museum, an art gallery, craft shops and other amenities. An official reopening on 3 July 1976 heralded a new era for this fascinating reminder of Halifax's earlier industrial heyday.

Location: Piece Hall is situated between Market Street and Charles Street, close to the railway station and parish church.

SOBERING REMINDER OF AN EARLIER FORM OF PUNISHMENT

Halifax Gibbet

The dramatic outline of the Halifax Gibbet serves as a salutary reminder of the days when capital punishment was meted out in public settings. In fact the gibbet was a guillotine and although formal records were not kept until 1541 it seems that it was first used in Halifax in 1286 when John of Dalton was put to death. During the period 1541–1650 a total of forty-nine people were executed in this manner.

A series of apparently minor offences could result in a trip to the gibbet. 'If a felon be taken within the liberty of Halifax . . . either handabend [with stolen goods in his hand], back barend [carrying stolen goods on his back] or confessand [confessing to the crime] to the value of thirteen pence half penny, he shall after three markets . . . be taken to the gibbet and there have his head cut off from his body.' In 1586 William Camden recorded that 'Halifax is become famous among the multitude by the reason of a law whereby they behead straightways whosoever are taken stealing.'

The reasons for Halifax's prolonged use of the gibbet are linked to the local cloth industry. One of the processes in cloth making involved stretching it out to dry on wooden tenterframes in open country where they were easy pickings for thieves. It is claimed that the extended use of the gibbet led to the plaintive statement 'From Hell, Hull and Halifax, good Lord deliver us'.

The only means of escape for a condemned man was by moving his head before the axe dropped and then making off across the parish boundary at Hebble Brook. Once out of the area the criminal was a free man unless he chose to return. It seems that at least one convict, John Lacy, made his escape this way but was executed some seven years later when he returned to Halifax.

Records indicate that the last victims of the guillotine were Anthony Mitchell and John Wilkinson from nearby Sowerby. Their crime was the theft of 16yds of russet-coloured cloth from tenterframes.

The gibbet was subsequently dismantled and the base fell into disrepair. During 1839 workmen who were tidying the area unearthed the skeletons of two men with severed heads. Speculation suggests that these were the remains of the gibbet's final victims.

During 1974 a 15ft high replica was erected on the original site at the lower end of Gibbet Street, while the original blade has found a place in the Calderdale Museum in the Piece Hall.

Location: The gibbet is sited on open ground at the lower end of Gibbet Street, above Burdock Way.

HALIFAX

Wainhouse's Tower – Arguably the Finest Folly of All

This slender structure located on the western outskirts of Halifax must rank as one of the finest follies in the whole country. Alternatively known as Wainhouse's Folly or the Octagon Tower, it was erected by John Edward Wainhouse (1817–83) during the early 1870s and resulted from the requirements of the Smoke Abatement Act of 1870.

At that time John Wainhouse owned a dye works in Washer Lane and the requirements of the new legislation meant that smoke from industrial premises in the Calder Valley had to be carried high above areas of housing. During 1871 Isaac Booth produced plans for a chimney that would be fed with factory

smoke through a pipeline. Three years later Wainhouse sold the works to his manager who declined to shoulder the considerable cost of completing the chimney. It thus remained under the ownership of John Wainhouse who decided to adapt it into a tower which he planned to operate as a 'general astronomical and physical observatory'.

This impressive tower was completed in 1875 with design work by Richard Swarbrick Dugdale at a total cost of £14,000. This slim tower soars some 275 ft above ground level and the topmost section is made up of a whole cluster of piers, pinnacles, balustrades and curving gables.

Inevitably perhaps, construction of Wainhouse's Tower has been linked with an ongoing quarrel between Wainhouse and magistrate and industrialist Sir Harry Edwards. It has been suggested that he built the tower in order to watch Edwards' movements more closely while the topmost ornamentation was a further attempt to incite his opponent. Feuding between the two local notables escalated from 1873 and in 1876 Wainhouse began to issue a series of pamphlets attacking his adversary.

John Wainhouse's eccentric tendencies spread to rather humbler structures. In Scar Bottom a terrace of cottages was decorated with mottoes and ornate Gothic porches, and properties in Wainhouse Terrace were given a frontage featuring balconies and supporting colonnades.

Location: Wainhouse Tower is adjacent to the A646 close to its junction with the A58 in the King Cross area of western Halifax.

TOPSY-TURVY TERRACES ABOVE THE RIVER CALDER

Industrial Workers' Houses at Hebden Bridge

Terraced housing takes many forms. Regency houses in Clifton, Bristol, represent the most stylish of terraces but later terraces in northern industrial towns were packed together as tightly as possible in a back-to-back formation.

Hebden Bridge lies in a deep hollow where Hebden Water joins the River Calder. The steep hillsides dictated that homes for the workforce at local mills and foundries could not be built in the usual manner. Instead they were constructed in a bottom to top layout, so that the houses were actually built on

top of each other. This style gave rise to the term 'flying freehold' because one occupant becomes dependent on his neighbour for the upkeep and sometimes even the structural integrity of his own house. When these rows of houses were built in West Yorkshire it was never thought that they would be sold individually and often they have roofs, cellars, bedrooms and stairways reaching into, over and under next door's property. Each row of workers' houses ended with a larger property to accommodate the foreman.

Location: Hebden Bridge is 6 miles west of Halifax via the A646.

WHIMSICAL ATMOSPHERE IN THIS FORMER WEAVING CENTRE

Heptonstall

It could be the hilltop setting or the range of unexpected architectural features that contribute to the whimsical atmosphere around Heptonstall's streets and passageways. The old church was founded around 800 years ago but most of the gaunt ruins that we see today date from the fifteenth century.

Just beyond the porch of the old church is the grave of David Hartley, the so-called 'King of the Coiners'. He was hanged at Knavesmire, York, in 1770 because of his involvement with counterfeiting at nearby Cragg Vale.

To the south of the old church is the new church of St Thomas. Built as a replacement for its near neighbour in 1854, its severe Victorian outlines serve to highlight several of the village's older properties.

The distinctive pale stonework of the Cloth Hall in Towngate dates from the mid-sixteenth century and was the place where local handloom weavers sold their cloth to dealers. The old grammar school was founded in 1642.

Heading along Northgate, the date 1578 is prominent on the large lintel stone of Whitehall Archway, and tucked away just below the roadway is the octagonal-shaped Methodist chapel. Opened in 1764, it is one of the oldest Methodist chapels still in use.

Panoramic views across the valley to the east of the church emphasise the enduring appeal of this former industrial community.

Location: Heptonstall is 7 miles west of Halifax via the A646.

SCHOOLING AND PLACE OF DETENTION UNDER ONE ROOF

Luddenden

It is not easy to understand the reasoning behind putting a school and lockup in the same building, but that is exactly what was done at Luddenden near Halifax. A large stone-built structure on the sloping roadway through Luddenden, dating from 1825, housed the village schoolroom on the upper floor while ground floor cells fronted on to the highway.

A single word is carved over each of the two roadside doorways – 'Warley' and 'Midgley' – and as the boundary between these two parishes ran through the middle of the building it seems that wrongdoers were deposited in the appropriate cell.

The cells have not been used for some time and the school moved to new premises in 1993, leaving new owners to find an innovative use for this building that combined schooling with custody.

Location: Luddenden is 6 miles west of Halifax on the A646.

A PINNACLED OBELISK

Stoodley Pike

Visible from miles around, this 120ft-high pinnacled obelisk boasts an interesting history. During 1814, following the surrender of Paris, local landowners made plans to erect a commemorative obelisk to mark the end of the Napoleonic Wars. Public subscriptions allowed building work to get under way but the project halted when news reached the Todmorden area that Napoleon had escaped from Elba.

Victory at Waterloo in 1815 brought a resumption of work and the finished monument comprised a curious mixture of a base with a chunky column supporting a tall cone. On 8 February 1854 this strange obelisk collapsed and a local newspaper, the *Halifax Guardian*, reported on the 'evil omen', which coincided with the news that the Russian ambassador had left England before the outbreak of the Crimean War.

Local leaders laid plans to construct a replacement obelisk and a new monument was completed in time to celebrate the signing of the peace treaty between Britain and Russia. Designed by a local architect James Green, the new obelisk was the same height as its earlier counterpart but rather different in appearance. It had eight sturdy buttresses supporting a balustrade which in turn underpinned an obelisk. Total costs amounted to £812 and an inscription gives details of the monument's history: STOODLEY PIKE: A PEACE MONUMENT ERECTED BY PUBLIC SUBSCRIPTION. Commenced in 1814 to commemorate the surrender of Paris to the Allies and finished after the Battle of Waterloo when peace was Established in 1815. By a strange coincidence the Pike fell on the day the Russian Ambassador left London before the declaration of war with Russia in 1854, and it was rebuilt when peace was proclaimed in 1856. Repaired and lightning conductor fixed 1889.'

Location: Stoodley Pike is 2 miles south-east of Todmorden. A bridleway from Mankinholes (south of Todmorden) runs north-east to the monument.

4

FORMER WEST RIDING LOCATIONS

A LONG CHURCH AND A REMARKABLE GRAVESTONE

St Andrew's Church, Kildwick

The village of Kildwick nestles in the valley of the Aire some 5 miles north-west of Keighley. While buildings such as the seventeenth-century hall and grange range along the hillside, it is St Andrew's Church in the heart of the settlement that attracts more attention. Known as 'The Long Church of Craven', it has an astonishing length of 170ft and width of just 50ft.

Arcades run like a long stone avenue from east to west without a chancel arch to break the sequence of ten bays on each side. Western sections of the arcading date from the fourteenth century but most of the rest of the church, including the tower and clerestory, dates from the Tudor period.

St Andrew's was visited by Charlotte Brontë during her time as a governess for Mary Wainman of Stonegap in nearby Lothersdale. Links with the Currer

family led to Charlotte Brontë adopting the *nom de plume* 'Currer Bell', to the great consternation of her publisher.

In the churchyard is a remarkable gravestone which has been carved with the features of an organ. It marks the final resting place of John Laycock, an organ builder, who died in 1889 at the age of eighty-one. His amazing tombstone is said to be a copy of the first organ that he built.

Location: St Andrew's Church, Kildwick, stands between the River Aire and the Leeds–Liverpool Canal, some 5 miles south of Skipton via the A629.

MEMORABLE MEMORIALS IN THIS RURAL CHURCHYARD

St Lawrence's Churchyard, Fewston

St Lawrence's Church is tucked away among wooded hillsides on Blubberhouses Moor, above the waters of Swinsty Reservoir. Its unusual features date from 1697 when it replaced earlier buildings on the site. The interior, with nave and aisle under the same roof and arcade supported by short columns, is matched by an equally intriguing exterior.

Few churchyards have seventeenth-century memorials but a box tomb on the east side of the church displays the date 1613. It has an extremely thick top and an earlier form of the letter 'j' in the inscription.

Other tombstone inscriptions show very fine linked lettering rather than the more usual separate letters and an unusual headstone from the 1750s has an

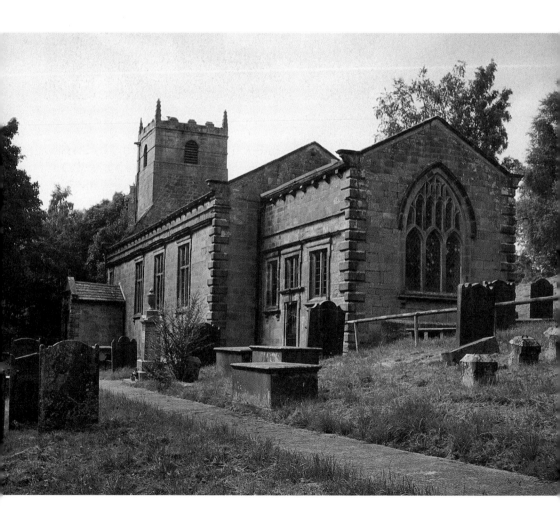

unusual low-slung headstone which looks rather like wooden stocks. The best-known tombstone is to be found near the quaint porch. It records the burial of Joseph Ridsdale's son on 30 February 1802 and of Joseph himself on 29 February 1823 but, of course, neither day ever existed!

Location: Fewston parish church is 5 miles west of Harrogate on the south side of the A59, close to the Swinsty and Fewston reservoirs.

A WEIGHTY METHOD OF CLOSING THE CHURCHYARD GATE

Lychgate at St Wilfrid's Church, Burnsall

Set in a glorious stretch of Wharfedale among grassy moors and fell sides, Burnsall has many charming features but perhaps the most curious of all is the roadside lychgate at the entrance to St Wilfrid's churchyard.

The nearby church has fragments of an older building, including fourteenth-century windows in the south chapel and a section of a Norman pillar in the north arcade. Fragments of Saxon crosses and sections of hogbacks (carved stone sculptures which may have served as grave markers) are on display within the church and a tub-like font dates from the second half of the eleventh century.

The lychgate probably dates from the late seventeenth century and turns on a central pivot. It is closed automatically by a heavy stone weight suspended on a cable in the side wall.

Location: St Wilfrid's Church is on the east side of Burnsall about 12 miles north-east of Skipton via the A59 and B6160.

RELICS THAT SURVIVED TWO ROUNDS OF VICTORIAN REBUILDING

A Large Bell in the Porch at Low Bentham

Low Bentham is mentioned in the Domesday Survey (1086) as 'Benetain'. A church from this period was destroyed by Scottish raiders after the Battle of Bannockburn in 1314. A new church was constructed from about 1340 and the tower is still standing, but much of this medieval building was destroyed in a further round of rebuilding in 1822.

By 1876, weaknesses resulting from poor workmanship some fifty years before led to another programme of reconstruction. Fortunately the rector at the time, the Revd Frederic Walker Joy, was an active Fellow of the Society of Antiquaries and he secured the safekeeping of a number of interesting artefacts. These included an ancient coffin slab, a Saxon crucifix, a memorial stone (inscribed with the name Kirkbeck – a nearby monastic house) and a stone corbel, but most curious of all is a huge bell. It was transferred from the floor of the tower into a new porch after this was completed in 1891. Huge and cumbersome, it still displays superb craftsmanship from the fifteenth century. Local tradition maintains that the bell was removed from Sawley Abbey but there is no supporting evidence. It hangs from roof timbers of the porch, and it has been suggested that it may be unique. Inscribed around the bell is the text '*SUM ROSA PULSATA MUNDI MARIA VACATA*' (When rung I am called Mary the Rose of the World).

Location: St John's Church, Low Bentham, is on the south-west side of the village.

CARE FOR THE POOR AND NEEDY IN THE ROUND

Beamsley Hospital

Early hospitals were primarily charitable homes for the elderly and infirm, and examples of these almshouses are found in many towns and villages, but Beamsley Hospital is highly unusual.

This low two-storeyed conventionally designed row of cottages stands close to the busy A59 with a central archway leading through to a garden. Within this tranquil setting there is a most unusual single-storey circular stone building with a stunted little tower in the centre and four chimneystacks. Under the central tower, which has lantern lighting, is a tiny circular chapel with seven rooms opening off it.

These circular rooms were originally occupied by seven needy women whose only route in or out of the building was through the chapel. This arrangement was no doubt intended to reinforce observance of the strict set of long-standing rules.

The hospital was established in 1593 by the Countess of Cumberland (as indicated on a tablet over the door) and 'finished more profusely' in the 1650s by her daughter Lady Anne Clifford. These finishing touches included construction of the front range and the addition of basic furnishings in the chapel and almshouses.

Beamsley Hospital continued to offer accommodation for needy women until the 1970s when ownership passed to the Landmark Trust.

Location: Beamsley Hospital is on the east side of the A59, about 6 miles east of Skipton and close to the bottom of Beamsley Bank.

A RANGE OF SURPRISES IN AND AROUND THIS DALES MARKET TOWN

Settle's Folly, Castlebergh and Victoria Cave

There are echoes of an earlier industrial era around the central marketplace and adjacent side streets at Settle, but close at hand are a number of man-made and natural surprises.

The Naked Man Café occupies a prominent position on the eastern side of the market place and down the years the curious carving on the frontage has attracted plenty of discussion. The building was originally an inn and the date 1622 is included alongside the motif. Closer inspection indicates that the figure

is not actually naked, as a shield covers his midriff, and buttons (shown as tiny black dots) suggest that he was in fact wearing a coat. Local folklore claims that the figure is meant to illustrate plain dress as opposed to more opulent clothing of the time.

A rocky outcrop overlooking the west side of the town, Castlebergh, is reached from the town centre by a woodland trail. The pathway bends and twists up the slope, and during the Edwardian era swing-boats were installed as a holiday attraction part of the way up the ascent. Local tradition suggests that in the days before the summit was covered in woodland a large sundial was set up on the flat area with numbered rocks arranged round the perimeter. Old paintings are said to support this claim but some local researchers dispute the existence of a sundial.

Within yards of Settle marketplace is a remarkable building known as The Folly, or Folly Hall, with the date 1679 inscribed on the lintel. Standing three storeys high, it has features of the 'Gothic survival' style of architecture set around a central doorway which includes twin Gothic arches and curious curved pillars. The main section of the building is more traditional with many mullioned windows set amid the impressive stonework.

It has been claimed that the reason for naming it The Folly was that the builder, Richard Preston, ran out of money and had to leave his curious structure unfinished, but this is rather different from the true facts. Preston was a tanner by trade. He died in 1703 after living in Tanner Hall, as he had named it, for more than twenty years. The Dawson family owned the property for around 250 years, but never actually lived in it, and the name 'Preston's Folly' originated during the eighteenth century. After standing empty for some time in the 1990s, part of the building was taken over by the North Craven Building Preservation Trust for use as a museum. At the time of writing (2007) the museum opens on a limited basis and the other portion of the building is privately owned.

On the upland slopes above Settle is a striking range of cliffs which contain a number of caves. Victoria Cave lies at a height of about 1,400ft above sea level at a location known as Kings Scar and consists of three large chambers with a single entrance facing south-west.

This amazing cave was discovered accidentally in 1838 and detailed investigation by members of the British Association some thirty years later uncovered a whole range of animal bones as well as a stag antler harpoon. Experts believe that early settlers had moved into this area from northern Spain by about 10000 BC.

Location: The Naked Man Café is on the east side of the marketplace. Castlebergh is reached via the lane on the north-west side of the marketplace and The Folly is prominent beside the roadway on the same side of the centre. Victoria Cave is accessible via a footpath from the west of Settle, but the interior of the cave is unsafe and members of the public are advised not to enter.

CURIOUS ARCHITECTURAL STYLES AND A MASTERPIECE FOR CANINES

Gisburn Park's lodges, hospital and dog kennels

Gisburn Park covers land beside the River Ribble, some 10 miles west of Skipton, and contains a set of structures with a whole range of contrasting architectural styles. The main building, Gisburn Hall, is the ancestral seat of the Lister family, Lords of Ribblesdale, and although William Dobson (writing in the mid-nineteenth century) stated that 'the house has no pretension to architectural elegance' its strength and solidarity serve to highlight the architectural features of other properties on the estate.

The lodges at the entrance to the park are covered in tiny castellations and the nearby railway tunnel has entrances embellished with massive turrets and glowering battlements. There is no trace now of another curious building in the estate grounds, a temple folly, but the most amazing set of dog kennels is to be found on the edge of the estate.

Standing on the banks of the River Ribble, the kennels are said to date from the late eighteenth century and may well have been built to house otter hounds. Thomas Lister (1752–1826) became Lord Ribblesdale in 1797 and was a keen huntsman. The estate soon became popular among the hunting fraternity and one vicar of Burnley, who was also the estate manager at Gisburn, was said to have been far more at home hunting than in the pulpit.

The dog kennels are an extraordinary structure and may well be unique in Britain. A classically proportioned central area is formed by a double cube measuring about 18ft in width with a vaulted roof supported by brick piers. An arch spans the eastern wall and on either side is a circular tower with domed brick roofs rising two storeys in height. A short set of stone steps links a ground-floor room in the north tower with an upper room.

This remarkable structure is now ruined and overgrown but is a prime case for preservation and restoration.

Location: Gisburn Park is 10 miles west of Skipton on the north side of the Clitheroe road. The main building is now a private hospital and the dog kennels are located on a separate private estate with no access to the public.

A MUCH TRAVELLED MASTERPIECE OF TIME-KEEPING

Memorial Clock at Barnoldswick

Before the advent of modern timekeeping devices, clocks and the clock-making industry had many an interesting phase of development but few can have had quite such a chequered history as the splendid memorial timepiece that was installed at Earby Methodist Church in Riley Street.

In its original position, fingers on the black and gold dial were driven by a clock movement that was bolted to the wall of the gallery in the church. The clock was made by John Pickles, a master engineer from Barnoldswick who was skilled in making a range of instruments from microscopes to telescopes. He wished to make a memorial for his former master with whom he had served his apprenticeship and built the clock for the church where his mentor was a devoted member of the congregation.

On a brass plate beside the clock was the inscription:

> In Memoriam to Henry Brown, Master Mechanic of this
> parish, 1848–1903; also Elizabeth his wife. This clock was
> installed by their family, made by his apprentice,
> John A. Pickles, and given as an appreciation of a good
> master and an able craftsman.

The chapel was bought by George Preston in July 1960 and subsequently demolished, although the adjacent Sunday School room remains.

At this point the clock was removed and installed at the engineering works of Henry Brown, Sons & Pickles Ltd at Wellhouse Mill in the nearby township of Barnoldswick.

In 1981 the company was taken over by the engineering firm of Gissing & Lonsdale Ltd and the clock was transferred to their premises in Wellhouse Road. It was subsequently fitted with two extra matching dials and fitted into a tower on the roof of the main office.

An information panel inside the entrance to the office reads: 'This clock, until 1988, had to be wound manually but by 4 April 1988 electric winding gear had been fitted, so eliminating any frustrating physical effort by male staff.'

One is left wondering if master engineer John Pickles would have approved of this refinement for the relief of a hard-pressed male workforce, but no doubt they marvel at his clock-making skills and remain intrigued by the travels of this remarkable timepiece.

Location: Gissing & Lonsdale Ltd are based in Wellhouse Road, Barnoldswick.

INDEX